Desperate Crossing

It was too dangerous to stay any longer. Eliza had to cross the river now or she would be captured. She stood up with Caroline in her arms. She nodded her silent thanks to Rosetta and George and raced out the cabin door toward the river.

With a sinking heart, Eliza realized that there was even more water between the massive ice chunks. She looked back at the cabin, then at the river path in either direction. There were figures in the distance hurrying toward her. Her eyes followed the river to the other side.

"It not that far," she whispered to Caroline, trying to encourage herself. "And when we get there, we gonna be free."

Eliza stepped onto the ice.

ALSO BY DOREEN RAPPAPORT

American Women
Their Lives in Their Words

The Boston Coffee Party

Trouble at the Mines

Doreen Rappaport

ESCAPE FROM SLAVERY
Five Journeys to Freedom

Illustrated by Charles Lilly

HarperTrophy®
A Division of HarperCollinsPublishers

Escape from Slavery: Five Journeys to Freedom
Text copyright © 1991 by Doreen Rappaport
Illustrations copyright © 1991 by Charles Lilly
Typography by Joyce Hopkins

Library of Congress Cataloging-in-Publication Data
Rappaport, Doreen.
  Escape from slavery : five journeys to freedom / by Doreen
Rappaport ; illustrated by Charles Lilly.
    p.   cm.
  Includes bibliographical references.
  Summary: Five accounts of black slaves who managed to escape to
freedom during the period preceding the Civil War.
  ISBN 0-06-021631-X. — ISBN 0-06-021632-8 (lib. bdg.)
  ISBN 0-06-446169-6 (pbk.)
  1. Fugitive slaves—United States—Juvenile literature.
2. Underground railroad—Juvenile literature.   [1. Fugitive slaves.
2. Underground railroad.]   I. Lilly, Charles, ill.   II. Title.
E450.R24   1991   90-38170
973'.0496—dc20   CIP
                                                                AC
First Harper Trophy edition, 1999
Visit us on the World Wide Web!
http://www.harperchildrens.com

for Luther Seabrook
and his family

Contents

FOREWORD

Slave escapes occurred from the earliest times after enslaved Africans were first brought to America in 1619. Without particulars of geography, and with only the North Star to guide them, slaves found their own routes across swamps, rivers and mountains toward the North and freedom. They went to the black quarters of Northern cities. There free blacks helped them to find jobs and shelter and to begin life over again as free men and women.

The Fugitive Slave Act of 1793 allowed owners to seize runaways and bring them to court to reclaim ownership. Slaves were not permitted trials by jury nor allowed to have witnesses speak on their behalf. Abolitionists—antislavery activists—attacked the law as unconstitutional and as legalizing kidnapping. By the 1830s abolitionists had created their own informal network to help runaway slaves. This network was called the Underground Railroad. Its "freight" or "passengers" were the fugitives. People who helped the fugitives, leading them to safety and often offering them transportation in rowboats, wagons, or other conveyances, were "conductors" or "stationmasters." "Stations" along the way—barns, attics, storerooms, secret rooms, and even straw mattresses—were places where the fugitives were fed and sheltered. As soon as possible, the freight was moved farther on the "railroad line" by wagon, by boat, or by train to the next station on the way to freedom.

It is estimated that 25,000 to 100,000 slaves escaped despite the overwhelming odds against making it. These are but a few of the stories of those courageous, ingenious Americans who risked their lives for freedom.

ESCAPE
FROM SLAVERY

The River of Ice

—◆—

"We need the money, and Eliza'll fetch a good price. She's young, and a good looker and a good worker."

Eliza's master's words stunned her. He was selling her. Not that she hadn't always known it was a possibility. Like all slaves, she lived with the gnawing reality that at any moment she could be sold and uprooted from her loved ones. But Eliza's owners had always been so kind to her that she had lulled herself into forgetting reality. Their kindness had vanished with their need for money. Within a few days Eliza would be separated from her two-year-old daughter, Caroline.

She knew what she had to do. She couldn't

let anyone take Caroline from her. She couldn't lose this child. She had already buried two others.

She waited patiently all day for the darkness and the quiet. She had done her chores efficiently but not too efficiently, not wanting to draw attention to herself. She had listened to her mistress' talking, ignored what she was supposed to ignore, nodded where she was expected to nod and answered when she was expected to answer. She had carefully controlled her every facial gesture and tone of voice so she wouldn't give away her angry feelings, so that her owners wouldn't suspect that she had overheard their plan to sell her.

Now it was almost time. Caroline was asleep, wrapped in a blanket made from saved scraps of wool. Eliza was tired too, but she didn't dare sleep. She needed to leave a few hours before daylight so she could cross the river when it was light. If she gave in to her weariness, she might not get up in time. She lay awake, thinking about the journey ahead.

When she thought it was time, she scooped

4

Caroline up from the floor and took her in her arms. "Be good, darling, don't cry now," she whispered, worried that the other children and the adults in the cabin would awaken.

She tiptoed out of the cabin. When she stepped outside, the night air bit into her face. She pulled the blanket farther over Caroline's head and looked up at the sky. There was the single star, the one that pointed the way to freedom. She followed it down to the other stars, grouped together like a drinking gourd.

"If I thirsty before I cross the river to freedom, I drink from the sky." She laughed silently at her joke.

There was no sound but her feet quietly touching the cold ground as she walked the five miles through the woods toward the river. She knew all about the river, the long, narrow river that separated the slave state of Kentucky from the free state of Ohio. She'd heard stories of slaves who swam or rowed across it. Eliza had dreamed of crossing that river ever since she was old enough to realize she was a slave. She had talked with other slaves about what it would be like to be free, but she had never thought she would be brave enough to escape. But all that had changed today. Today, with her master's words, she had found a courage she hadn't known she possessed.

Crossing would be easy. The river was always frozen over at this time of year. Her feet, clad in thin-soled shoes, were cold now and would be even colder by the time they touched free ground, but that was a small price to pay for freedom. She pulled Caroline closer and ran along the narrow path that led to the river.

In less than two hours, at daylight, she spotted the river. She raced eagerly toward it. When she reached the riverbank, she saw that the ice had started to thaw. It was broken up some and was slowly drifting by in large cakes. Her heart sank. Crossing was impossible now. She would have to hide and wait for the cold night wind to swoop down and freeze the water some more.

Her eyes searched in both directions for a sign of shelter, for a place where she might rest while she waited for the river to freeze again. She had heard there were free colored folks living along the river who helped runaways. There were a few cabins in the distance. But how would she know which cabin held friends? She wouldn't, but she would have to take a chance.

She pulled the blanket away to reassure herself that Caroline was still sleeping. "Thank you, Lord, for keepin' her still." Then she ran down the path alongside the river. It was a while before she came to a small cabin, not much bigger than the cabin that she had shared with ten others. Black smoke was rising out of its chimney. Dared she stop and ask for help? Her eyes scanned the landscape again. There was no place to hide near the river. And no place in the woods. And even if she could find a place, Caroline might not survive in the freezing cold. What choice did she have? Her master would soon discover she was gone and start tracking her down.

She lifted her head to the sky. "Dear Lord, help me."

She knocked gently on the cabin door. No answer. She knocked again more vigorously. The door opened hesitantly. A short man, with frizzy gray hair and skin black as ebony, nodded at her. It was the kind of gentle greeting black folks often gave each other on their way to Sunday service.

"Mornin'," he said in a quiet voice. His friendly eyes fixed on the bundle that was her daughter.

Eliza swallowed and whispered, "We need a place to stay till nightfall."

"Welcome," he said, hurrying her into the one-room cabin. The cabin had a small table, two chairs, and straw matting on the floor near the hearth to sleep on. There was a roaring fire in the hearth.

"I'm George, and that's my wife Rosetta." His wife, a pleasant-looking woman with cocoa skin like Eliza's, was stirring something in a large pot over the fire. She beckoned for Eliza to come and sit near her.

Eliza squatted down on the straw and held Caroline gently in her lap, hoping not to disturb her sleep. Rosetta ladled out a liquid from the pot and handed it to Eliza. The broth was warm and nourishing. George brought Eliza a blanket and told her to stretch out. Before she knew it, she was asleep. She spent most of the day sleeping by the fire.

When she awakened, it was almost twilight. George was gone. Rosetta was feeding soup to Caroline. Eliza waited until Caroline had sipped the last spoonful. Then she took her daughter in her arms, planted kisses all over her face, and rocked her back and forth. Caroline drifted into sleep again.

"Where are you from?" Rosetta asked. Eliza told her story. Rosetta told Eliza that she was a freeborn colored but George had been born a slave. She had worked hard and saved the money to buy his freedom.

"But if you free, why you stay in Kentucky?" asked Eliza.

Rosetta smiled gently. " 'Cause there are more like you, wantin' to cross the river. And they need shelter till they get cross. So we stay and wait and help."

The door opened, and George hurried in.

Eliza knew from his worried eyes that she was not safe. "The slave hunters are out. Goin' from cabin to cabin askin' about you."

It was too dangerous to stay any longer. Eliza had to cross the river now or she would be captured. She stood up with Caroline in her arms. She nodded her silent thanks to Rosetta and George and raced out the cabin door toward the river.

With a sinking heart, Eliza realized that there was even more water between the massive ice chunks. She looked back at the cabin, then at the river path in either direction. There were figures in the distance hurrying toward her. Her eyes followed the river to the other side. "It not that far," she whispered to Caroline, trying to encourage herself. "And when we get there, we gonna be free." She looked upward to the sky. "Lord, we need you." She took Caroline's arms and wrapped them around her neck. "Hold on tight, and don't let go, 'less I tell you," she whispered.

Eliza stepped onto the ice. It was solid. She

stepped across a large chunk onto another. That was solid too. And then another. She rushed forward to the next chunk. The ice was giving way. She could feel the weight of her body threatening to pull her down into the water. She leaped onto another chunk. Cold water came rushing up to her ankles.

On the other side of the river she saw a man standing at the shoreline. Eliza leaped onto another chunk. And then another. "We gonna get there," she said to herself as she felt the water rising above her ankles.

A minute later the water reached up to her knees. "Lord, Lord." Soon the water would start to cover Caroline. She was only thirty feet or so from freedom. The water rushed up to her chest.

"Mama, mama," Caroline screamed as the water began to cover her.

"Let go, baby." With her left hand Eliza undid Caroline's arms from around her neck. With her right hand she grabbed a chunk of ice. Then she slid Caroline onto the piece of ice. Caroline screamed louder as the ice touched her back. "I here, baby," Eliza shouted, grabbing the ice chunk with both hands and kicking her feet hoping to propel herself and the ice with Caroline on it farther toward the shore.

She was only ten feet or so from the shore. Caroline's screams filled Eliza's ears. The icy water was beginning to numb Eliza. "Lord, we so close." She kicked even harder. The chunk of ice with Caroline on it was almost at the riverbank. Eliza was only a couple of feet from shore. The man grabbed Caroline off the ice, and Eliza pulled herself onto the shore.

Eliza's pursuers watched passively from the riverbank on the Kentucky side as she and her daughter stepped onto free soil. The man at the riverbank took Eliza and Caroline to the home of antislavery sympathizers, who gave them food and dry clothing. That night Eliza and her daughter began their trip by the Underground Railroad to Canada.

Free Like the Wind

Every muscle in Dosha's neck and shoulders ached. He looked down from the tree at his horse, Free, wondering how he was faring after two hours. Free had been his father's horse, before his father was killed two years earlier in an accident cutting stone. Dosha had named him Free because his father had never stopped thanking the Lord that he was born free instead of a slave. Dosha still missed him, but when he galloped over the fields with Free, it was like having part of his father with him.

Dosha squinted his eyes and scanned the horizon. It was hard seeing. The sun, moving down to meet the earth, no longer warmed the air, but its strong rays obscured the details in the distance.

It was a week since folks in Cabin Creek had gotten the news that slave hunters were around, tracking down the Jackson girls. Selena Jackson was eleven, a year older than Dosha. Her sister, Cornelia, was a couple of years younger. Dosha didn't much like girls, but these two were different from most. He had to admit that. They'd made their way to Cabin Creek, Indiana, from somewhere in Tennessee, over two hundred miles away. Hiding in thickets and caves during the day. Scrounging for food in barns, eating pig slop to keep from starving. They had traveled in the pitch black of night, crossing mountains and swamps. Their only guide had been the North Star. He didn't know how they'd done it, and had to admit that he wasn't sure that he could have.

Folks in Cabin Creek were used to slave hunters coming after runaways. The black settlement was just north of a six-mile stretch of wilderness that had been leveled by a tornado. Many slaves lost their pursuers in this tangle of huge, downed trees and thick underbrush and ended up in Cabin Creek. Hounds couldn't follow the human scent when escaping slaves waded in the swamp or ran above ground, jumping from fallen limb to fallen limb. When the runaways got to Cabin Creek, folks hid them until they could get them farther north to Canada.

Cabin Creek was only one of about twenty rural black settlements in Indiana. Slavery was forbidden in the Indiana Constitution, so free blacks and freed slaves immigrated here. Around fifteen years earlier, in 1826, Dosha's parents and other free blacks from North Carolina had come to Cabin Creek. They'd drained the boggy land that white settlers didn't want. They'd turned it and tended it until the soil was rich enough to yield plentiful harvests. A group of white Quakers, who had also immigrated from North Carolina, raised money to tide the black community over until it was self-sufficient.

Now Cabin Creek had over a hundred residents. It also had a whole system worked out to help runaways. Dosha's watch duty was only one part of the system.

Dosha blinked his eyes at a flurry of motion about a mile or so away. Definitely riders. He waited another minute hoping to distinguish how many, but he couldn't make it out. They were getting closer. He scampered down the tree, mounted Free and kicked him hard. Free broke into a gallop almost immediately. A bullet from a shotgun whizzed by. Dosha's heart jumped like a scared rabbit. Another shot. He kicked Free harder.

In the center of town Dosha pulled in Free's reins, put a horn to his lips, gave a loud blast, then galloped off to a secluded spot about a quarter mile away. His friend Samuel was already there, with his horse. Dosha left Free with him and ran back to the center of town.

When Bessie Watkins heard the horn, she ran to the window. Four men on horseback were riding straight toward her cabin. There was no back door or back window to the cabin, and the men were too close to risk letting the girls out the front door. *How did they find out?* she thought. There hadn't been any strangers around Cabin Creek for weeks, and it was unthinkable that anyone in town might have given them away. She rummaged through a drawer to get the clothes she'd saved for just this occasion.

By the time the four men stopped in front of her cabin, about fifty townsfolk had already gathered. They formed a semicircle around the slave owner and the others, and then fanned out the length of two cabins on either side of the Watkins cabin. Dosha, standing near the front of the crowd, saw the glint of the sheriff's badge as he dismounted from his horse. The other three men stayed on their horses. "Watkins, it's the sheriff," he shouted.

Bessie Watkins opened the door, a long shiny knife in her left hand. "I'm assuming you want my husband. He's not here," she said defiantly.

"No matter," the sheriff replied. "Got a writ here that gives me the authority to search your premises for stolen property."

18

"And what might that property be?" Her strong voice wavered a bit.

"Two of my slaves," shouted the slave owner, dismounting his horse. The man stood a head taller than the sheriff, with big broad shoulders and thick arms. His hands were large and swollen around the knuckles.

He looks more like a man who hauls things than a man who whips others to do his hauling, thought Dosha.

Bessie Watkins held up the knife for an uneasy moment. "Don't know about no property, but do know that anyone crossing here, will be cut in two," she said, plunging the knife into the door-jamb for emphasis.

Isaiah Watkins stepped out of the crowd and walked up to the door of his mother's cabin. Dosha knew Isaiah as a gentle man—unless he felt wronged or angered. Then he could be meaner than a polecat. "Now, sheriff, what's this here fuss you stirring up that's disturbing my mama?" His words came slow and stiff, as if talking was an effort he wasn't used to. It was all part of the plan.

"Got a writ here," said the sheriff, reaching into his pocket, "that gives me authority to search her premises for stolen property."

"Mighty fancy language," said Isaiah playfully. Then his voice turned stern. "But what does it mean?"

Dosha's aunt and his cousins, who were about Dosha's size, wended their way to the front of the crowd. When they neared Dosha, his aunt didn't even glance at him. She led her children toward the Watkins cabin.

"Sheriff," the slave owner shouted, "don't explain nothing to that nigger. That woman's got my girls."

"What woman you talking 'bout?" Dosha's aunt spun around and glared at the slave owner. "I ain't got your girls. These two are my boys, or ain't your eyes good enough to see that they're boys?" She pulled off the wide-brimmed hats covering her sons' faces and turned the boys around to face the slaveholder. The crowd laughed.

Bessie Watkins pulled the knife out of the door-jamb, and Dosha's aunt shooed her children into the cabin. Then she turned her head and shouted at the slave owner, "Maybe you should look 'round and see if there's a hole in the ground nearby where they been let down to the Under-ground Railroad." The crowd responded with more laughter.

The sheriff thrust a paper into Isaiah's hands. "Read it yourself."

Isaiah brought the paper close to his eyes and moved his eyes and one finger word by word across the paper, pretending that like a child, he still struggled with his letters.

Isaiah's wife led their two boys out of the crowd toward the cabin. When they were about halfway there, the slave owner hollered, "Where are those people going?"

Bessie Watkins plunged her knife into the doorjamb again. "Here. My *friends* are always welcome in my home." Her voice was still defiant but a bit shaky.

Isaiah stopped reading, pulled the floppy hat off one of his boys and turned him around for the slave owner to see. Then he pulled the hat off his other boy and turned him around too. "Just wanted to confirm for that there man that you were boys, too."

The crowd's laughter was punctuated by a piercing whinny from the slave owner's horse. The angry man cracked his whip at the horse's neck to silence him, then snapped the whip on the ground. For the first time, Dosha felt scared for Cornelia and Selena.

Isaiah reached the bottom of the page. His eyes and finger darted to the top, and he began reading again, as if he didn't completely grasp what he had read.

Another woman led her son toward the cabin. Dosha followed behind them.

"Well," said Isaiah finally looking up at the sheriff, "I don't see where this here paper say that you have the right to enter my mama's house."

The sheriff grabbed the writ and hurriedly read it through. Then he handed it back to Isaiah, pointing to the paragraph that authorized the search.

Isaiah's earnest eyes studied the paper again. "But this here is a writ to find property. I don't know of any laws in Indiana that say human beings is property. Human beings is human beings. Property is houses and land. Proving that people is property would be a difficult job for anybody . . . even a fast-talking lawyer."

"I can prove it, all right. I have my right to them under the law." The owner's mounting frustration brought scattered laughing from the crowd.

"I doubt that," said Isaiah. He leaned over, shielding part of his mouth with his hand, and whispered to his mother.

Her eyes flashed. He whispered something else to her. Her eyes reluctantly calmed down. She sighed and nodded.

Isaiah turned back to face the sheriff. "Sheriff,

I have proposed a compromise to my mama, and she has . . . uhum . . . graciously accepted it. My mama here say that you can search her premises, providing that if by any chance you do find two girls in her house, you give them a fair trial to determine whether or not they are these here . . ." He looked at the writ again.

"Jackson, Selena and Cornelia Jackson," shouted the slave owner. His frustration brought more laughter from the crowd.

The cabin door opened. Dosha's aunt and his cousins walked slowly out of the cabin. *Hurry up*, Dosha thought. *We're running out of time.* Dosha and the other boy brushed past them and entered the cabin. In the middle of the room stood two boys and Selena and Cornelia. Barefoot, dressed in faded rolled-up pants, baggy shirts and floppy hats, the girls looked like boys.

Dosha heard Isaiah acknowledge the slave owner with a big "Thank you, sir." Then he addressed the sheriff. "Well, I doubt that these here Cornelia and Selena Jackson are here, but you are free to look."

Bessie Watkins stepped away from her door. As the sheriff and his men rushed past her, Dosha and the girls walked right past them out the door and back into the crowd. They walked slowly amid the pine trees to the bushes. Laughter gurgled up inside Dosha as he pictured the slave-owner rifling through the cabin, opening cupboards, slamming doors, pulling up mattresses, and swearing more and more as he realized that his search had led him nowhere.

Samuel was waiting near the bushes. Dosha helped Cornelia and Selena up onto Samuel's horse. "Gentle now," Dosha whispered into Free's ear as he swung his leg over Free's back. Dosha didn't want either horse galloping. Noise traveled. Free obediently led the way slowly through the bushes to the road out of town.

When they were about a mile out of town, Dosha leaned over again and whispered to Free, "Come on, boy, don't let me down," and Free took off like the wind.

Selena and Cornelia were taken twenty miles away, where they were hidden for a few weeks until the slave owner abandoned his search. Then they were sent by Underground Railroad to Canada.

A Shipment of Dry Goods

Henry Brown sat on a wooden stool that was too narrow for his large body, slowly separating tobacco leaves from their stems. Most mornings the past fifteen years, he'd sat on this stool in the factory in Richmond, Virginia, separating the leaves, moistening them with fluid, then pressing them into lumps. Fourteen hours a day in the summer, sixteen in the winter. Henry's master had Henry work in a factory because he needed the money Henry made more than he needed him on the plantation. Henry paid his master two hundred seventy-five dollars a year from his wages and was allowed to keep the rest.

One hundred twenty out of the hundred fifty

workers in the factory were slaves hired out by their masters. Slaves were a good investment. You could always earn back what you paid for them, and then some, by hiring them out.

Henry's wife, Nancy, was owned by another master. Her master hired her out as a house servant. But Nancy's earnings didn't satisfy him, so he demanded that Henry pay him fifty dollars a year if he wanted Nancy to live with him. Of course, Henry had to feed and clothe his family too. The four of them lived in a sparsely furnished one-room cabin. With the garden plot that Nancy had painstakingly carved out in front of their cabin, they had enough food. Most importantly, they had each other.

In their twelve years of marriage, Henry had even managed to save some money, hoping someday to buy his family's freedom. But now he knew that plan had been a fool's dream. He would spend the rest of his days on this stool, fighting off boredom and pain. And the rest of his nights he would be alone in the cabin aching with sadness.

Yesterday morning, when he'd left Nancy and

the boys to go to work, Nancy had hinted that she'd have a surprise waiting for him when he returned. It was August. The garden overflowed with okra and tomatoes. Henry loved the soft red fruit and crisp green vegetable smothered in onion sauce. The sauce was Nancy's mama's recipe. When he asked her how she made it, she always teased him that only the women in her family were given the secret.

Fourteen hours later, when Henry returned home, there was no sauce, no Nancy, no Joshua, no Ezekiel. They were gone. Hauled away to the auction block and sold to a man in North Carolina. Sold away, like his mama and sisters and brothers had been sold, never to be seen again.

Henry had run and begged his owner to buy them back. Henry had showed him the one hundred-twenty dollars he had saved over the years and pleaded with him to give him another eight hundred dollars or so to buy back Nancy and the children. His owner had laughed and dismissed him with "Dumb nigger, go to work and don't bother me no more."

Henry fled to the church to absorb Job's patience, Solomon's wisdom and Jesus' love and forgiveness. But nowhere in the Bible did he find a satisfactory answer for such injustice.

He returned home to wait for the morning, to wait to take his place in the hot factory on a stool suited for a child, not a man.

Henry stopped at the corner and peeked around it before he turned into the street. There was no one in sight on the city streets. At four in the morning he didn't expect there would be. And he knew he was safe if anyone were to question him. He had a pass from the factory overseer in his pocket. Whenever slaves ventured out alone, they needed passes signed and dated by their masters. The pass was proof that they had permission to be out, proof that they weren't trying to escape. But even with the pass, Henry didn't want to meet up with any white folks today.

He hurried down the empty street until he came to a sizeable store whose windows were filled with farm implements and supplies. A sign above the door read C. BULLIT, although the black man couldn't read it. It was too early for anyone to be out buying anything, but Henry looked through the store windows just in case.

He turned the knob on the front door. It was locked, just as Mr. Bullit had said it would be. He continued down the street, turned another corner, and made his way to the back of the store. That door was open as planned. He walked on tiptoe through the storeroom of unpacked supplies to a small room off the front of the store.

A man was leaning over his desk, his back to Henry, busily writing among a clutter of papers. Henry took a deep breath. "Mister Bullit, sir?"

The storekeeper turned around and acknowledged the greeting with a nod. He was a slender, middle-aged man. Long narrow face. Stern gray eyes. He put a finger to his lips, walked around his desk toward the front of the store, checked the lock on the front door and came back.

"Can't be too cautious, Henry." His Southern drawl was as thick as Henry's master's.

"No, sir," Henry answered quickly, as he always answered white men. Henry heard the back door open.

"Who's there?" the shopkeeper shouted gruffly.

"James Smith. We did have an appointment here today, didn't we?" A tall man the color of ginger, dressed in a fine suit that marked him as a gentleman, nodded to the storekeeper and eagerly grabbed Henry's hand. "Nice morning for a trip, brother."

Henry saw the storekeeper's eyes take in his friend's amber skin, thin nose and small mouth. James Smith was an educated free colored. He could read and write better than most white men, but Henry knew that Bullit saw him as just another nigger.

Henry's heart swelled with affection for his friend. In the last eight months there had been too many nights to remember when Henry had cried with Smith. Never thought he'd cry in front of another man.

It was Smith who had told him to consider escaping. He had told Henry that he was a conductor on the Underground Railroad, a network of people who helped slaves escape north. If Henry wanted to escape, he would help him any way he could. And Henry had come up with his plan.

James Smith's eyes rested on Henry's right hand, where the skin on two fingers was eaten away.

"Spill too much of that vitriol oil you give me on it," said Henry. "But it work good. My fingers worry Allen so much when he see 'em, he told me go right home and put a poultice on 'em. In the five years he been factory overseer, that man never give nobody a day off." Henry smiled and pulled a paper out from his pocket. "Gave me a pass for three days, too. So he won't be lookin' for me now."

"Do you want to see the crate?" the storekeeper asked impatiently.

Henry picked up the white man's impatience and nodded nervously. He had no illusions that Bullit was helping him because he liked him or because he believed slavery was wrong. Bullit was helping him because Henry was paying him good money. The two black men followed the storekeeper into another small storeroom. In the center of many unpacked boxes of goods was a wooden crate.

"As you ordered. Two and a half feet wide, three feet long, two feet eight inches deep."

Smith stared at the crate, then at Henry's muscular arms and large frame. Henry weighed two hundred pounds and was five feet eight inches tall. "How are you expecting to fit in there, Henry?"

Henry ran his hands over the rough pine planks. He lifted the lid of the box and slid his fingers over the baize lining. "I can take it for two days or so." He smiled at his friend. "And it sure beat walking two hundred and fifty miles."

"Maybe so. Maybe not," responded Smith. "But what will you do if they don't keep the crate upright? I know how careless these transport men can be."

"Nothin' to worry about," the storekeeper protested. "I'll be sittin' alongside Henry all the way to Philadelphia."

"What's the route?" asked Smith.

"We go by wagon to the Potomac, cross by steamer to Washington, then by rail to Philadelphia." Henry heard the resentment in the white man's voice. White men didn't like explaining themselves to black men, even if the black men were free.

Henry reached into his pocket and pulled out a tool, no bigger than his hand, with a screw point at one end and a cross handle at the other. He stepped into the box, bent his knees and sat down. It felt cramped already. He wrapped his arms around his knees and pulled them closer to his chest to get more room. "Okay, close it," he said, bending his head down.

Bullit slammed the crate lid down.

Henry pressed the tool into the top of the crate right over his head to mark holes for breathing. He turned the tool two times. Then he shouted,

"Open up." Smith's worried face greeted Henry when the lid was lifted.

Henry pressed the pointed screw into the lid again, slowly turning it around and around until it made a tiny circle, too tiny for anyone to see. And, possibly, too tiny to breathe through. He turned the screw three more times. The opening was a mite bigger, but he didn't dare make it any bigger or it might be seen. He made two other holes on either side of the first.

"You done?" the storekeeper asked sharply.

"Almost, sir." Henry pulled a shriveled object out of his pocket. "Mister Bullit, sir, if you kind 'nough to show me your bucket, I like to fill this here rabbit sack with water. That and a few small biscuits should hold me till I get up North." Henry filled the sack with water and tied it with a thin piece of leather.

"I'm goin' in my office now," Bullit said brusquely. "Adams'll be by about seven. You two stay here." It was an order.

Two hours later Henry Brown embraced his friend and stepped into the box. Bullit closed the lid, nailed up the box and tied it with the hickory hoops on each end. With a large grease pencil Smith wrote on the crate:

To: W. H. Johnson
Arch Street
Philadelphia, Pennsylvania

THIS SIDE UP WITH CARE

Without a word to Smith, Bullit went back to his office and waited for the men from Adams' Express. James Smith took a last look at the crate and left the store by the back door.

"Got an order for a pickup from Bullit."

"In there." The storekeeper pointed to the storeroom without looking up.

"Take that side. I'll take it here, Frank. Ready? . . . Lift."

Mr. Bullit didn't look up as the two men hoisted the crate through his office, out the back door and onto their wagon. A few minutes later one man returned with a written receipt. The storekeeper took it without reading it.

Henry felt the crate being slid into the wagon. The driver slapped the reins, and the horse trotted along the streets. Not as bouncy as I expected it would be, thought Henry.

After a while the clopping stopped.

A pickup. Henry assumed his crate would be pushed around some to make room for others.

The men left the wagon and returned in a few minutes.

"Thought they said there was only two small boxes to pick up."

"That's what Horace told me."

"How we gonna fit these three in?"

"Complaining won't help." The wagon shook a bit as the two men jumped up onto it. "Stand this one up and make more room."

They hoisted Henry's crate up and left it standing on its side. His head and back were jerked farther down. His hands loosened from around his knees. His bent knees stiffened. *If the box topple over, my head split open. Mr. Bullit, tell 'em to put me back right.*

He heard mumbling and heavy breathing as

the men loaded other crates onto the wagon. "Is that the way that crate's supposed to be?"

"Don't know. Don't care."

The balls of Henry's feet burned. His knees felt permanently locked. His back ached. With each clipclop of the horse, he bounced up and down, hitting his head. Then he realized that Bullit had broken his word. The white man wasn't going with him to Philadelphia.

At the office the men unloaded the wagon, turned the crate on its right side and then disappeared. Stillness surrounded Henry.

For the next two hours Henry tried to keep his mind off his frozen muscles and joints by silently reciting Biblical psalms:

The Lord is My Shepherd; I shall not want.
He maketh me to lie down in green pastures:
He leadeth me beside the still waters.
He restoreth my soul. . . .

Loud voices interrupted his silent recitation. The crate was hoisted up again and put onto another wagon. The horse picked up its trot.

Henry pressed his fingers against his knees and clicked off the horse's rhythm to time each bounce and prepare for its jolt. Suddenly his mouth felt dry. He slid one hand carefully into his pocket and pulled out the water sack, but did no more than wet his lips.

The wagon continued its bumpy journey. Henry gave up focusing on the horse's rhythm and returned to his silent recitations:

The Earth is the Lord's, and the fulness thereof; the world, and they that dwell therein. . . .

A few hours later the wagon stopped again. Henry assumed they were at Potomac Creek, where the crate would be loaded onto a steamer for Washington, D.C. He was hoisted up, carried a ways and set down, this time upside down.

He managed to wedge his hands under his head, so he could rest more comfortably. Then he realized that the air holes were under him now. Would any air get in? His eyes began swelling as if they would burst from their sockets. The veins in his temples throbbed. He tried to lift his head up a little but couldn't move it. He felt flushed, then cold.

My God, my God, why hast thou forsaken me? . . .

Henry fainted. When he awakened, he was soaked in sweat and had no sense of how much time had passed. After a while he heard a man say, "I'm tired of standin.' Been over two hours now. I'm gonna get me something to sit on." The man turned Henry's crate right side up and sat down on it.

Gradually the pressure in Henry's eyes and temples subsided. His heartbeat returned to a normal rhythm. He rubbed his hands over his knees and thighs to soothe the stiffness. He wiggled his toes until he could feel them.

Praise the Lord with harp: sing unto him with the psaltery and an instrument of ten strings. Sing unto him a new song; play skilfully with a loud noise.

He celebrated his good fortune with a few sips of water and a few nibbles of a biscuit.

At Washington, D.C., the crate was loaded onto a wagon and taken to the rail depot.

"Ain't enough room in this car. Let's send this one through tomorrow."

Please Lord, don't let 'em be talkin' 'bout me.

"Can't. It came by express. It's gotta go on."

Henry heard the door of the luggage car close. The men's voices faded away. It was dark, but quiet. He felt protected by the stillness around him. He sipped more water and prayed the trip would be over soon.

James Miller McKim kept out of the ring of light cast by the kerosene lamp hanging on a wooden post and watched the workers unload the freight from the railroad cars. One crate after another. None seemed big enough to hold a man.

McKim was a member of the Philadelphia Vigilance Committee. Militant black and white abolitionists in Philadelphia had created the society to aid runaway slaves. The abolitionists offered the fugitives whatever they needed—food, shelter, clothing, medicine, money, and legal advice. They helped them get to the next stop on the Underground Railroad to New York, Boston or Canada.

McKim had received many a telegram that dry goods (the code for men) or hardware (the code for women) were on the way. Tall black men dressed up as women had appeared at his door. Friends had brought runaways in wagons built with false drawers. But never before had he been informed that a man was being shipped in a box by railway express. He thought it a foolish plan to send a man this way without air to breathe. Not that he would have discouraged the man from doing it. Despite his white skin, James Miller McKim believed that slavery was another form of death.

He saw three men place a box about eight feet long on the platform. He walked toward the ring of light. The workers were still emptying the box-car. "Anything from Richmond, Virginia?" McKim craned his neck, trying to read the address on the long wooden crate. He was looking for a box that was addressed to W. H. Johnson. The box was addressed to someone other than McKim to avert suspicion.

"Anything from Richmond?" a man called out to another man, standing about ten feet away. The man scanned his work orders and shook his head no. McKim returned to the side and watched for another hour as the rest of the freight was unloaded. There wasn't any box the right size. McKim went home.

That afternoon he received another telegram from Richmond, saying that his shipment of dry goods would arrive the next day. Worried that a second appearance at the station might bring too much attention, he hired a driver he knew to bring the crate directly to his house.

Henry didn't know what time it was or how long he'd been wherever he was. All he knew was how close and foul the air was, like a sultry August night in Richmond when there wasn't a whisper of a breeze. He'd taken a chance and used the tool to enlarge all three holes, but it hadn't helped much. There didn't seem to be much air out there to breathe.

He flexed his fingers and toes and felt nothing. He rubbed the tops of his knees. No feeling there either. His bent back was so stiff, he didn't think he would ever be able to straighten it up. He'd finished his biscuits, and his water sack was almost empty, but his throat and lips were so parched, he had to have some water. He untied the sack and dipped his fingers into it. He dabbed a few drops of water on his forehead and put the sack up to his lips and savored the last few drops.

Suddenly the door of the luggage car opened, and a strange male voice said, "It's in here, Dan." Henry's crate was lifted up and carried for some distance, then gently put down as if the bearer was concerned about the contents. He was outside in the fresh air.

He heard the man command his horse to get going, and the horse trotted off at a leisurely pace. Dared he hope this was the last lap of his journey?

After a short while the wagon stopped. He was lifted up again, taken up some stairs and placed on a floor.

"Thanks, Dan," said a male voice. Henry heard other male voices talking. Where was he?

A few minutes passed. Someone rapped quietly on the lid of the crate. "It's all right now."

Henry answered faintly, "All right here, too."

"Thank God, he's alive," the man shouted.

"Open it up," urged another insistent voice. The hickory hoops were cut. Henry welcomed the noise as the nails were pried out.

When the lid was lifted, Henry saw a blur of faces. He closed his eyes quickly, then opened them slowly to get accustomed to the daylight. His eyes met the pleased eyes of a man with skin as dark as his. Henry felt giddy with happiness. He scanned the faces of the other men in the room. They were white. Momentarily he felt scared. Then he remembered. James Smith had told him that there were some white men up North who protested against slavery. His journey to freedom was over.

"How do you do, gentlemen?" he asked, his voice stronger.

"We do just fine," answered the black man. "What about you?" He grabbed Henry's hands to help him up out of the box.

"Just . . ." Henry fainted. Two other men ran over to help lift him out of the box and carry him to a couch. Henry smelled something funny under his nose and slowly opened his eyes and smiled. "Guess I not feelin' good as I thought." Everyone waited for him to speak again. Henry rested for a while, then sat up and shook hands with each man as he introduced himself.

When the introductions were over, he smiled and said, "I told m'self if'm lucky 'nough to live, I thank the Lord, and so I will."

And in a rich baritone voice, he recited the fortieth psalm from the Bible:

"I wait' patiently for the Lord; and he
incline' unto me, and heard my cry.
He brought me up also out of an horrible
pit, out of the miry clay and set my feet
upon a rock, and established my goings.
And He hath put a new song in my
mouth, even praise unto our God: many
shall see it, and fear, and shall trust in the
Lord."

Henry Box Brown, as the liberated slave was affectionately nicknamed, recuperated from his arduous journey and then went on to Boston. He spoke of his daring escape at antislavery meetings throughout the northeast. With the help of a friend he wrote a book about his life and escape; it sold 8,000 copies in two months. In 1851, upon the passage of the Fugitive Slave Law, which stated that runaway slaves found in free states had to be returned to their owners, Brown left for Canada. Encouraged by Brown's success, *James Smith shipped two other slaves north, but they were caught. Smith was arrested and imprisoned for seven years for aiding the runaways. At his release, he was honored at a mass meeting in one of Philadelphia's black churches.*

Pretending

Jane pretended not to listen to what her master was saying as she poured the coffee from the silver urn into the delicate china cups. Slaves were always pretending around white folks. Pretending not to hear, not to think, not to feel, not to care.

Jane's biggest show of pretending was last year, when Colonel Wheeler told her he was selling her oldest son. When she heard the words, words she'd feared hearing since Lucas was born, her head felt loose from her body, and her legs shook so she was sure she'd collapse. But she knew that wouldn't do. So she pressed her shaking knees together, hid her trembling hands in her pockets, and pulled her chest cavity in tight until her whole body felt like stone. She forced the tears back into her eyes.

For the last half hour Colonel Wheeler had been boasting to his father-in-law, Mr. Sully, about his life as United States minister in Nicaragua. "Sure it's hot down there. But not hotter than Virginia summers. And we have a big beautiful mansion. And plenty of servants." He sipped his coffee. "That's why I sold all ours. Except Jane here. Millie just wouldn't let her go. She's used to her and her ways.

"Not that she's completely trained," Colonel Wheeler continued. "Why, that uppity nigger told me she wouldn't go to Nicaragua without her two boys. Surprised me, too. She didn't seem to care at all last year when I sold her oldest one, Lucas. I was planning on selling the other two before we left. Could get a good price for them. But your daughter said to take them along. Said Jane's boys would be better trained than those Indian boys in Nicaragua."

The colonel laughed. Mr. Sully watched Jane pick up the tray with the coffee urn, and when she pushed open the kitchen door, he turned to his son-in-law and whispered, "It's dangerous taking Jane up north. Northerners think slaves are automatically free once they're past the Mason-Dixon Line."

"I have no choice." Colonel Wheeler made no attempt to lower his voice. "There's only one boat going to Nicaragua, and it's leaving from New York. Anyway, Jane has no reason to run away. She has it good with us. She doesn't work in the fields. All she does is lay out your daughter's clothes, dress her and brush her hair."

Jane didn't need to turn around to know that her master had sucked in his cheeks until the hollows made his face look cadaverlike, and pursed his lips tight until his mouth shriveled up like a fish's. Next he would force his eyes into slits, and then point the forefinger of his right hand at his father-in-law, as he always did when he was being his most arrogant, and continue boasting about how good he was to Jane.

She put the tray down in the kitchen. *Keep pretendin'*, she told herself. *Soon you be free*.

Colonel Wheeler stepped down from the carriage and impatiently signaled Jane and her sons to step down too. Ever since their train had pulled into Philadelphia twenty minutes ago, and he had found out they were too late to catch the two-o'clock steamboat for New York, he had hovered over her. How would she ever slip away from him to get help?

"Stay here," his gruff voice ordered when they were halfway across the lobby of the Bloodgood Hotel. As he hurried to the large reception desk, Jane's eyes swept the mahogany-paneled lobby for a colored face. None. She craned her neck to get a better view into the dining room. Black men scurried back and forth with trays of food. She felt somewhat reassured. She looked back at her owner. The man behind the desk was pointing up. The colonel nodded, then hurried back toward her. "I'm going in to dinner." He guided her and the boys toward the large mahogany staircase.

Jane's youngest son tugged at her arm. She hushed him with a look. He hadn't eaten since early this morning, but she wasn't going to worry about that now. Her older boy knew better than to hope for some food just because his master was eating.

"Now remember," Wheeler said, placing Jane and her boys on a small bench on the second floor overlooking the lobby. "Don't talk to any colored folk. And if anyone speaks to you, tell them you're a free colored traveling with a minister." Jane clasped her hands and smiled, staring blankly off into the distance, like Mrs. Wheeler in that picture in the parlor. Colonel Wheeler hurried down the stairs.

It wasn't but a few minutes before he came back and cautioned her again not to talk to anyone.

"But why would I?" she whispered, resuming the pose of before. His tense eyes relaxed. He went back downstairs to eat.

A cinnamon-colored woman came up the stairs. Jane leaned forward in her seat and whispered, "Sister, I a slave." Jane's throat felt like it was going to close forever. "My master told me not to speak to no colored folk. Told me to lie that I free, but I not. But me and my chillun wanna be."

"You poor thing," the woman said, walking away. Jane didn't call after her.

An ebony complexioned woman, carrying a stack of towels, walked up the stairs. "Sister," Jane whispered as she neared her. She nodded but didn't stop.

Maybe I should grab the chillun and get to the street. But what if there no coloreds there either to help us?

The woman, her hands now empty, walked back past her. "Sister . . ." Jane raised her voice. "Sister."

"Good afternoon, sister."

Jane rejoiced silently in the ease with which the woman greeted her. "Me and my chillun slaves. We wanna be free." Her voice trembled, but it was strong.

"How long you gonna be here?"

"Till five o'clock. Then we takin' the boat to New York."

"Nellie!" a sharp voice called out from the bottom of the stairs.

Nellie raised her hand to acknowledge the greeting. Then she turned back to Jane. "Don't worry. I'm gonna help you." She hurried down the stairs without looking back.

It was four o'clock in the afternoon. William Still undid his collar and the top two buttons of his shirt and rolled up his sleeves. The hot, humid air had soaked his body. How he would love to close up the office and go home. He brushed the indulgent thought out of his mind. There was just too much to do. Every day more and more slaves showed up in Philadelphia. Needing a place to hide. Needing to find their way to Canada. They usually found their way to the Vigilance office. The least he could do was stay here and be ready to help.

William Still had been born a free man, but his parents had been born slaves. His father had bought his own freedom with money he saved from being hired out. His mother had attempted escape twice. The second time she took two of her children with her, leaving two behind. She always said, "Better two with me than four in slavery." But when she said it, her eyes clouded over like she was getting ready to cry.

The Stills eventually bought a forty-acre farm in Medford, New Jersey, about twenty miles from Philadelphia. William and his thirteen siblings worked hard to keep the farm going. They didn't have much time for school, but William made up for his lack of formal education by reading.

Eleven years ago, when he was twenty-three, he had moved to Philadelphia. He'd worked for the Vigilance Committee for eight of those eleven years. He started as a janitor and now headed the committee. The Fugitive Slave Act, passed five years before, stated that slaves were property and must be returned to their masters even if they escaped to free states. Federal marshals were instructed to seize all fugitives and any citizens helping them, even in the free states. It was much more than one person could possibly do, but Still did the best he could for all the fugitives needing protection. He also interviewed them and wrote down their stories. He wanted his people to have a record of their courage. In addition, the record might help them find other family members who passed through Philadelphia to freedom.

"Note for Mr. Still."

"Who's it from, son?" he asked the slender boy about ten years of age.

"Don't know sir. Just was told to bring it here."

Still took the note and read:

MR. STILL—*Sir: Pleze cum to Bloodgood's Hotel soon as possable—three slaves here want liberty. Their master is taking them to New York.*

The note was unsigned and undated. "When did you get this note?"

"About a half hour ago, sir. A colored woman told me, get here fast. And I did."

William Still gave the boy loose change from his pocket. "Good job, son." Before the boy knew it, Still was out the door and on his way to see Passmore Williamson. Williamson was secretary of the Philadelphia Anti-Slavery Society and worked closely with Still to help runaway slaves.

"I can't go with you now, William. I have business in Harrisburg that I must prepare for." Passmore Williamson saw the disappointment on his friend's face. It would be easier for William with the white man along. Easier if he talked to the slave owner. Easier if he fielded the inevitable hostile remarks by other whites. Though Pennsylvania was a free state, and Philadelphia's abolitionist movement was well established, most white Philadelphians didn't accept free black men like William Still as equals. And just as many didn't think slaves deserved to be free.

"But here's what you should do," Williamson continued. "Go down to the hotel. Find out the name of the slaveholder and the slaves. We'll telegraph ahead to New York and help them when the steamer docks there."

William Still hailed a carriage to take him to the Bloodgood Hotel. "I'm looking for three colored folks." He spoke softly to the black bellboy at the hotel entrance. "I think they're slaves."

"Saw a tall, dark woman with two boys, being took by a white man to the wharf."

"How long ago?"

The bellboy shrugged his shoulders. "Not too long."

"Then we'd better hurry." William Still heard the familiar voice of Passmore Williamson. He turned around to greet his friend. "I thought you needed me more than my clients in Harrisburg did," Williamson continued. He saw how pleased Still was to see him.

The two men raced around the first deck of the steamer. No tall dark woman with two boys was in sight. On the upper deck on a long bench sat a tall black woman. Her hair was pulled tight over her ears and wrapped in a bun at the nape of her neck. Her hands were clasped in her lap. Her eyes looked down, like she was getting ready to pray. Two boys sat on one side of her. On her other side was a well-dressed white man.

William Still moved cautiously toward the woman. She looked up. He nodded at her. He wasn't surprised by the flash of fear in her eyes.

No matter how much a slave wanted freedom, the moment of confronting her master, the moment of asserting that she was leaving, was usually frightening.

"Sir, I'd like to speak to your servant," Mr. Williamson addressed the colonel.

He looked up. "If you have anything to say to her, say it to me," he snapped.

Mr. Williamson turned to Jane. "I want to tell you of your rights, ma'am." The white man's gentle voice made her feel unafraid.

"She knows her rights," interrupted Wheeler.

"Do you want to be free?" Williamson ignored the interruption.

"I do, sir, but I belong to this here gentleman, so how can I be free?"

"You're in Pennsylvania now," he said. "Our laws say that once you're here, you're free. As free as he is . . ."

"She understands all about the laws making her free," Wheeler interrupted again. "She knows perfectly well she has a right to leave if she wants to, but she doesn't. Jane is going on a

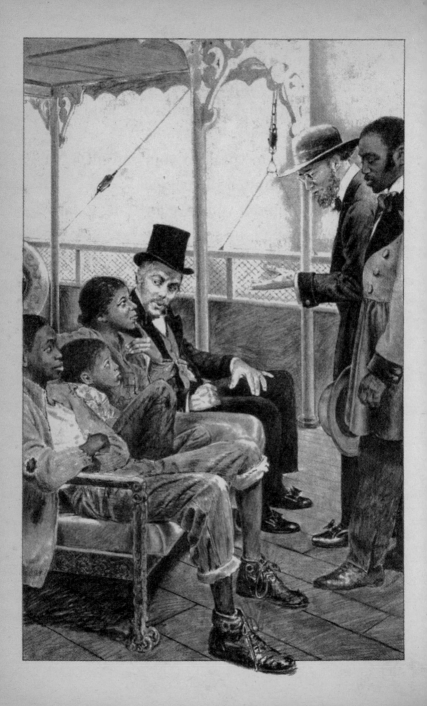

visit to New York. Afterward she and her children are returning to Virginia." He paused. "You wouldn't want her to go with you and abandon her children, would you, sir?"

Jane remembered the colonel's cool, unconcerned voice telling her that she would not be allowed to even say good-bye when Lucas got sold.

"And she doesn't want to be interfered with . . ." Wheeler insisted.

Jane interrupted, "I not free, but I want freedom. . . . Always wanted to be free . . . but he holds me."

Colonel Wheeler's eyes opened wide like a schoolboy about to tell his mama a fancy story about why he hadn't done something he promised to do. "Well, Jane, if you want to be free, I'll give you your freedom. I've been planning to do it for a long time anyway."

Jane smiled to herself. *Guess white folks good at pretendin' too.*

The last bell before departure tolled.

"It's time." William Still offered Jane his arm.

She rose and, putting her arms around her children, told them to get up too. Wheeler grabbed her arm and jerked her back to the seat. Jane tried to wrest free from his grip, but it was too strong.

Suddenly two black men appeared, picked up Jane's boys and carried them to the stairs leading to the lower deck.

"What are you doing?" Wheeler shouted, and let go of Jane.

She rushed toward the stairs. Wheeler lunged at her and grabbed her by the wrist. But this time Williamson interfered. He took hold of Wheeler by the collar and held him to one side so Jane could pass.

"Leave them alone; they're his property!" yelled a passenger.

"Come back here, Jane!" cried Colonel Wheeler as she hurried down the stairs.

"Massa John! Massa John!" the youngest boy cried out.

"Your mama's gonna regret this!"

Wheeler wrested free from Williamson but

could not get down the stairs, for three black men formed a chain at the bottom.

Jane's boy was still crying as William Still helped her into a carriage. "Foolish boy, cryin' so after Massa John," she scolded. "He sell you in a minute if he catch you."

As the carriage pulled away from the wharf, Jane clicked her tongue in rhythm to the slow *clip-clop* of the horses' hooves. She didn't need to turn around to know that her master, Wheeler, was screaming and pointing his finger at the white man who spoke so gently.

It was Jane's third day of freedom. She'd spent all three days in the home of James and Lucretia Mott. The Motts were Quakers and staunch abolitionists. Lucretia Mott had helped found the Philadelphia Female Anti-Slavery Society over twenty years ago and was a well-known public speaker against slavery. Their house was one of the stations on the Philadelphia branch of the Underground Railroad.

Jane thought the Motts were kind, gentle people. They gave her good food, and plenty of it. And a nice firm bed with soft sheets to sleep in. Jane had never slept in such a bed before. Hard to believe white people could be so nice.

But she still felt frightened. She kept trying to pretend to herself that she wasn't, but she knew she would be somewhat afraid until she was safe in Canada. Mrs. Mott had told her that the final arrangements would be made by tomorrow. Soon she and the boys would be truly free. Her heart dropped thinking of Lucas. She'd never see him again. But at least her other two would grow up free men.

The parlor door opened. Jane jumped up to greet Mrs. Mott.

"Pray thee, sit down." Lucretia Mott walked to the straight-backed chair opposite Jane.

Jane relaxed in her chair.

"Jane dear, I've come to ask thee to do something important . . . and dangerous."

Jane saw concern in the white woman's eyes.

"Thy master has caused much trouble." A chill passed over Jane. "He had Mr. Williamson put in prison because he says he doesn't know where thee is. And now the judge has charged the five colored men who helped thee at the steamer with rioting, kidnapping, and assault. If they're convicted, they could be put in jail for a long time." She paused. "They need thy help."

"How?"

"By coming to court and testifying that thee was not kidnapped. By swearing that it was thy decision, and thine alone, to leave Colonel Wheeler."

"But coloreds not 'lowed to testify 'gainst white folk."

A slight smile showed on Mrs. Mott's face. "They are in Philadelphia," she said.

"Then why it dangerous?"

"Well, according to the laws of Pennsylvania, all slaves are free once they step foot on our soil. But the federal government has a different law. That law says that all slaves must be returned to their masters, no matter where they are. There's a federal marshal in Philadelphia who's sworn that if he finds thee, he'll return thee to the colonel. If he finds out that thee is in court, he might come there and try to arrest thee. We'll be there to protect thee, but we can't guarantee what might happen."

Jane's heart beat faster. "What happen to Mister Williamson and the others if I don't testify?"

"I don't think it'll go too well for them. Colored men aren't that well liked in the North, either. And neither are white abolitionists, like Mr. Williamson."

"The court believe me over Mister Wheeler?"

"I don't know. But it's their strongest defense."

"I do it."

Four days later, dressed in a plain black dress with a veil over her face, Jane walked into the county courtroom, accompanied by Lucretia Mott and another Quaker woman. Jane sat down near the front of the courtroom and tried to concentrate on what the lawyer was saying to the first witness, but she couldn't. Her eyes were riveted on the back of Colonel Wheeler's head. She wanted to run out of the courtroom. *Pretend he's not here*, she told herself. *Pretend you can't see him.*

After a few more witnesses had testified, the clerk called, "Jane Johnson."

"I here." She stood up and walked toward the witness box.

The clerk held a Bible in his hands and told Jane to put her right hand on it. "Do you solemnly swear to tell the whole truth and nothing but the truth, so help you God?" he asked.

"I do."

"You may sit down."

Jane sat down and pushed her veil off her face. Her eyes caught the colonel's, fixed on hers, like a conjure man trying to put a spell on her. She stared back at him, long and hard, to break the spell.

The lawyer got out of his chair and walked slowly toward Jane. "Colonel John Wheeler has sworn that you were kidnapped against your will by my clients. He has also sworn that these five men forced you to go with them. Is that true?"

"Nobody force me away. Nobody pull me.

71

Nobody lead me." She spoke rapidly, almost without a pause. "I went away of my own free will. Always wanted to be free. Planned to be free when I came North. Weren't sure it be in Philadelphia. Thought maybe it be in New York."

"Jane, how do you feel now that you're free?"

"Happy. Real happy. Chillun happy too."

"Do you have any desire to go back with Colonel Wheeler?"

She looked directly at her owner. His eyes were still fixed on hers. "I rather die."

When Jane finished her testimony, she walked out of the witness box. Lucretia Mott and the other woman met her as she approached the aisle and walked on either side of her toward the courtroom door. Jane knew this was the moment when she might be arrested. She knew she should be scared. It made sense to be scared. But she wasn't. She'd never felt freer in her life.

Jane got safely out of the courtroom.
A few days after the trial, she and her children

72

left Philadelphia by Underground Railroad for Canada. The jury had found all five men not guilty on the kidnapping and rioting charges. Two men were found guilty of assault and battery and were sentenced to a week in jail. Passmore Williamson spent over three months in jail. He was charged with contempt of court, for filing an evasive report in which he stated he knew nothing of Jane's whereabouts. After his release from jail, he continued to help other slaves find freedom.

"Two Tickets for Mr. Johnson and Slave"

Ellen looked up from her sewing, out the small window of the cabin at the fallen darkness. William had worked late into the night for over three weeks now. It seemed everyone in town wanted something built in time for Christmas. Ellen was working extra hard too. Mrs. Collins was having three dinner parties and wanted a new dress for each one. Ellen went back to her sewing, with one ear listening for William.

It was three years since they had met, two since they'd married. Ellen had known early on that William loved her and felt sure she loved him, but when he first proposed, she refused. "It's not that I don't love you, William—I do. But . . ." she had said.

"Then why not?" he had asked.

"Because we can't really pledge our love. It's not ours to say forever. We can't even marry without our masters agreeing."

Eventually Ellen agreed to marriage, but not to having children. "They won't belong to us," she argued. "They can be taken away at Dr. Collins's whim. It's too cruel to them . . . and to us."

Ellen and William lived in Macon, the largest town in the center of Georgia. They had different masters but were allowed to live together in a cabin in the woods, behind Ellen's master's mansion. The cabin was plain and simple, but it was theirs unless their masters changed their minds. Like other town slaves, William was allowed to hire himself out, providing he paid his master $220 a year. Whatever he earned above that, he kept. William was a good cabinetmaker, and over the last three years had earned about $150 over what his master expected. Ellen's nimble hands worked exclusively for Mrs. Collins, busily sewing party dresses for her. Theirs was a much better life than that of plantation slaves, but it wasn't freedom.

She heard William hurrying up the path, faster than usual. She put her sewing aside.

"Ellen." He spoke excitedly as he came through the door. "I got it." He sat down next to her on a wooden bench he had made from odds and ends of wood left over from various jobs. "Got a plan to escape."

Over the past two years William and Ellen had talked a lot about escaping, but couldn't figure out a plan that seemed possible. Macon was in the deep south. It was many hundreds of miles to freedom in the North—miles of forests to walk through, rivers to wade across, mountains to climb and bounty hunters to hide from.

William took her hands in his. "Christmas is in eight days. We ask Dr. Collins and Mr. Taylor for a three-day pass. Tell 'em we want to visit friends on the Smith plantation. Like we did last year. I sure they agree. We escape then."

"But how?"

"You gonna take me up North. Slave owners can take their slaves anywhere they want." He stroked her soft cheeks. Ellen's skin was as white as his was dark. Her mother was a slave, but her father was a white man. Her grandfather had been white too. "Finest belles in Macon want skin like yours. No one gonna think you colored."

"But white women don't go traveling with colored men servants."

"No one gonna know you a woman." He wrapped his arms around her waist. "You be dressed up like a gentleman—top hat and all. A sickly but wealthy invalid white man goin' to Philadelphia. Hopin' to find some cure up North for his many ailments. And of course traveling with his nigger." He raised his eyebrows, like his master did when he was dressing him down. "No self-respecting gentleman, well or sick, go travelin' without his nigger."

"But where will I get these fine clothes?"

"What we can't buy, you sew. If need be, you sew trousers and a shirt grand enough for the best hotel. I find you a pair of boots and polish 'em till you can see your poor, pitiful face in them." He laughed. "And pitiful it'll be. All wrapped up with a bandage."

"Like I'm suffering from a toothache?"

William nodded.

Ellen's mouth broke into a grin. "I'll pretend I'm deaf, too. Then I won't have to talk much."

"But when you talk," said Henry, "it be real fine. Mrs. Collins always boastin' that her girl Ellen talk as good as any white lady in town." He pulled her toward him and held her in his arms.

Ellen had been in the big house since she was eleven, listening to her mistress and her friends gossip away the day while she tied her corset, buttoned her shoes and fluffed out her petticoats. When Ellen grew older, she was taught to sew, and in between the pinning and the hemming she overheard the talk of the women. Her ears took in the cadences, the rises and falls, in their way of talking, and she spoke as they did.

"Do you think it'll work, William? Do you really think I could fool people?"

"With the help of the Lord, we can do it."

Ellen's master agreed without hesitation to give her three days' holiday over Christmas. William's master complied somewhat grudgingly.

Buying gentlemen's clothes was not as easy. Georgia had a law forbidding white men to trade with slaves without a master's consent. But William knew which merchants in town disobeyed the law and traded with anybody who had money.

He went to different parts of town, at different times of the day, and to different stores. He bought the linen shirt and morning coat from a shopkeeper he'd heard would sell a slave anything at the right price. He tricked another proprietor into believing he was buying a bow tie for his master. He bought the boots and socks from a house servant down the road. He couldn't find trousers small enough, so Ellen made her own, sewing long into the night, after she finished sewing for Mrs. Collins.

The night before they left, William polished the boots until they looked almost new. He cut Ellen's long hair off square in the back. She had no regrets as she wrapped the long locks up in a cloth and buried them in their mattress ticking.

Next morning, before the sun rose, Ellen slipped on the black socks. They were thin from wear. She stepped into the pants that she had so carefully stitched. The waist fit snug as she had planned, but the pant legs were baggy. She had deliberately made them that way to emphasize the impression of a frail gentleman.

She ran her fingers over the fine linen shirt. How beautifully made it was. No visible stitching around the collar or cuffs. The pleated front lay perfectly flat. Its small, even stitches looked more like decoration than necessity. She wondered how much William had paid for it.

"William," she whispered, waving the thin black tie. No one in the big house could ever hear their conversation, but this morning she wasn't taking any chances.

Out of the corner of her eye she watched William's large, muscular hands clumsily fold and refold the bow tie until it lay straight. His master had been right to have him trained to be a carpenter and not a house servant. She sat down on the bed and pulled up the boots. William had thickened the soles and hammered small heels onto the boots to give her more height. She walked around the room. Her feet weren't used to being so constricted. The leather rubbed slightly through the thin socks at both ankles.

No time to fuss now, she thought, putting on the black morning coat. She'd altered the shoulders to fit her better and tapered the sides slightly too, but left the jacket, like the pants, somewhat baggier than normal.

"How do I look?" She tucked her short hair under the top hat.

"Not finished yet." William handed her two large packets of herbs and meal wrapped in cloth. Ellen pressed the poultices to her chin while

William wrapped a long white cloth over them. He pulled the cloth more tightly as it neared the top of her head, and then pulled it down around the other side of her face and back to her chin. With a few wrappings her cheeks and chin were completely covered. The cloth felt tight, but she didn't dare loosen it. It would loosen up some of its own accord anyway. If it loosened too much, it would separate and reveal her beardless face.

The final touch was an arm sling. Ellen didn't want anyone questioning why she couldn't sign her name. She might talk like a white Southerner, but she had never learned to read and write. Georgia law forbade teaching slaves to read. Ellen was determined that once she got up North, she would learn. And then she would teach other black people to read too.

"Well, how do I look?"

"Sickly . . . but genteel," William answered.

He opened the cabin door and they peeked out. It was barely dawn. Everything was still. Ellen put on dark-green spectacles and walked out into the fresh morning air. They tiptoed up the dirt path, and where it met the road, they went off in different directions to the railroad station.

"Two tickets to Savannah for William Johnson and slave." Ellen lowered her voice as much as she could but still feared the stationmaster would know she was a woman. But he didn't even look up as he pushed the train tickets and some change toward her.

William helped his invalid master cross the platform and mount the steps to the first-class coach. Ellen handed him his ticket without looking at him, and he went off to find the car where slaves were allowed to sit.

"Can I help you, sir?"

Ellen showed her ticket to the conductor. He led her to a window seat. She knew she should give him a coin or two for helping her to her seat, but her hands were trembling so she didn't dare take money out of her pocket. She tried to distract herself by looking out the window.

"Fine morning, isn't it, sir?" said the man seated next to her.

It was Mr. Cray—Dr. Collins' friend. He'd known her since childhood. She'd seen him only two days ago when he'd come to the big house for dinner. *What's he doing here? Maybe they know we're here, and they've sent him to get us.*

"Fine morning, isn't it, sir?" Mr. Cray repeated.

If I talk at all, he'll know it's me, thought Ellen.

"Fine morning, isn't it, sir?" Cray said again.

The man opposite Ellen laughed. "I think he's deaf."

Ellen knew Mr. Cray wouldn't care if he was deaf or not. He hated to be ignored. Cray tapped her on the shoulder. She knew she couldn't ignore him. She turned and looked at him. There was no recognition on his face that he knew her. *Amazing how white folks can see us all the time and never see us,* thought Ellen.

Mr. Cray raised his voice and, almost shouting, repeated his greeting for the fourth time.

"Yes," she mumbled, then turned her face to the window.

"Great deprivation, being deaf," said the man opposite Ellen.

"Certainly is." Cray felt generous toward the young invalid now that he'd broken through his deafness. He lunged into conversation with the other man. Ellen closed her eyes, trying to block out his words, praying he wouldn't try to involve her in conversation again. Twenty minutes later, when he got off the train, relief washed over her.

No one bothered the young invalid on the rest of the ride to Savannah. When the sun was almost down, the train pulled into the station in Savannah. A horse-drawn omnibus took the passengers to a hotel so they could have tea and pass the hour until the ferry for Charleston left. Mr. Johnson didn't feel well enough to go inside the hotel with the other passengers, so his servant brought his tea out to the bus.

An hour later they were shuttled to the wharf. William took Ellen directly to her berth on the steamship. Then he went to the gentlemen's lounge to prepare the rheumatism medicine.

"Where's your master?" asked a young military officer.

"He turned in, sir." William hoped his voice didn't reveal how nervous he felt.

"What's wrong with him?"

"Not feeling well. Ain't been well for a long time."

"He did look like a sickly sort," said another passenger.

"What's in that pot?" the officer asked, as the smell of camphor filled the room.

"Opodeldoc, sir."

"What's it for?"

"Rheumatism. My master got a terrible case."

"From the way that concoction smells, I should call it opodevil," said another man, laughing at his own joke. "Get it out of here now, or I'll throw it overboard."

William took the warmed medicine to Ellen's berth. She didn't say much in the little time

William was with her, but he knew she was scared. He was scared too. He wanted to stay the night, hold her in his arms, reassure her, and himself, that their plan would work. But slaves didn't sleep with their masters in first-class berths. He kissed her good night and reluctantly left the cabin to search for a place to spend the night, for there were no sleeping accommodations for slaves. Near the bow of the boat he spotted a pile of sacks. He plopped down and felt warm air rising from a funnel behind. He closed his eyes and hoped no one would bother him till morning.

The next morning Ellen knew she could no longer postpone eating with the passengers without arousing suspicion. She felt worried. What if she couldn't pitch her voice deep enough to pass for a man? William helped the invalid to a seat at the captain's table.

"How are you feeling this morning, sir?" asked the captain.

"Better, thank you," she muttered.

"Well, I guess that awful-smelling medicine

that your boy heated up did some good," said the young officer who'd questioned William in the lounge.

Ellen nodded. William stood at her side and cut her chicken into bite-sized pieces.

"Eat up, sir, it'll do you good," said the captain.

They don't know I'm a woman. She felt some relief. She looked down at the chicken and rice on her plate. *Hands, don't tremble.* She picked up her fork and stuck it into a small piece of chicken. William went to stand along the dining-room wall, waiting for his master's next command.

"Your boy's quite attentive," said the captain.

The man seated opposite Ellen leaned forward on his elbows. "Now sir, if you'd like to sell that there nigger, I'll buy him." He speared a large piece of chicken with his fork. "Just name your price." He bit into the chicken like a hungry dog.

Ellen gauged her reply. "I couldn't sell him, sir. I can't get on too well without him."

"I'm a slave trader, and I tell you he'll do you

no good if you take him across Mason's and Dix-on's line." He shook the small uneaten piece of chicken on his fork at her. "He's a keen nigger. I can see from the cut of his eye that he's certain to run away. You had better sell him to me."

"I think not, sir. I have great confidence in his fidelity."

"Fidevil!" the slave trader shouted, banging his fist on the table. It hit the edge of his saucer, and his coffee spilled on the lap of the man next to him. The scalded man jumped up. The slave trader dismissed the accident with a "Sorry neighbor, but accidents will happen in the best of families."

A bell clanged.

"We're in Charleston," said the captain.

"Let's go up on deck," suggested the officer.

Ellen didn't want to go on the deck. She didn't want to be in such a public place, didn't want to be in public view. If their masters had guessed they were missing, someone might be out there looking for them.

"Master . . ." William was at her side. Without a word, he led her to the gentlemen's lounge. Only when the crowd on the wharf thinned, and most passengers had left the boat, did Mr. Johnson's faithful servant help him off the boat to hail a carriage.

"Where to, sir?" asked the driver.

"Best hotel in town, and hurry." The arrogance in Ellen's voice surprised her. The driver soon deposited them at the Charleston Hotel.

"Stand aside." The hotel manager rushed from behind the reception desk, pushed William out of the way and offered his arm to the sickly-looking man. He snapped his fingers, and a servant braced Ellen on her other side.

"Now, what can I do for you, sir?"

"I need a room. A quiet one."

"For how long?"

"One night."

"Barnabas, take the gentleman to Room Four. Daniel, help Barnabas." The man looked at Ellen's arm sling. "Sir, if you'll just tell me your name, I'll gladly register for you."

If only that man knew his fuss was over a nigger!

91

William fought an urge to laugh as he followed Ellen and her two helpers down the hall.

"He sure do think you one fine Southern gentleman." William began laughing as soon as the servants left them. Ellen pressed her hand over his mouth to stifle his laugh.

He playfully wrested her hand off his mouth. "No one can hear me."

"Can't tell," she whispered back. She took off her glasses and rubbed her eyes. "I'm so tired."

William knew how tired she was. Playacting every minute. Listening to her voice, watching her hand gestures, thinking about her walk. Worrying she'd give herself away with one wrong move. But he couldn't let her rest now. He slid off her arm sling, then unwrapped the face bandage. "You have to go to dinner, or that man gonna be suspicious."

She sighed. "All right."

William took the poultices and ran down the hall to the reception desk. "My master need these heated up."

The man rang a bell, and a slave appeared.

"Barnabas, go down to the kitchen and get these heated up right off. Then take them to Room Four." He turned to William. "You can go back. Barnabas'll bring them down."

In a few minutes Barnabas knocked at their door. William opened it just enough to be able to take the poultices but to prevent Barnabas from seeing in. He put them on the mantelpiece. When they cooled, Ellen pressed them on her face and William rewrapped the cloth around her face. She slipped on the arm sling and hobbled off to the dining room. William left her at the dining-room entrance as two servants rushed to greet her.

She gonna be eatin' some beautiful bird and I lucky if I get a few scraps, he thought, walking to the kitchen.

Ellen stood on the ticket line in the Charleston train station and looked around. William stood off to the side. The young military officer who had sat at her table on the steamer was two places behind her on the line talking to the steamer captain. The two men caught her glance and nodded. She returned the greeting, then turned away. The line moved forward. In a few minutes she was at the ticket window.

"Two tickets for Philadelphia, via Wilmington, for Mr. Johnson and slave." Her supposed name rang false in her ears.

The customs officer looked at her, then signaled William to come over. "Boy, do you belong to this gentleman?"

"Yes, sir."

The customs officer handed the tickets to Ellen and opened a large ledger. "Sir, I need you to sign your name and the name of your boy in this here book. And I need a dollar duty on your boy."

Ellen reached awkwardly into her pocket. "Here's my dollar, but you must sign for me. I can't do much writing with my hand wrapped like this."

"Can't do that, sir. Law wants your signature, not mine."

Her eyes darted nervously behind the dark glasses.

"Well, that's a silly law," bellowed the military officer, coming forward from his place in line. "I'll vouch for Mr. Johnson," he snapped at the customs officer as if dressing down a disobedient soldier. "Know his kin like a book, and I think, sir"—he pointed a finger at the man—"that you know me and my kin, so there shouldn't be any trouble here for my friend Mr. Johnson."

"I'll vouch for him too." The steamer captain was at her side. "Be glad to register this gentleman's name and take full responsibility." The captain took the book and signed it. Then he turned to Ellen. "It's all right now, sir."

"Thank you kindly." Her words came slow and stilted.

"Hope you don't think that he intended any disrespect, sir. We make it a rule to be very strict in Charleston. Got to. Too many damned abolitionists around who want to run off with our niggers." The captain offered his arm for Mr. Johnson to lean on.

The overnight trip to Wilmington, North Carolina, was uneventful. The next morning, when

95

they changed to a train for Richmond, Virginia, no one objected as the slave settled his frail master into an empty compartment that had a couch that was set aside for families and invalids.

Ellen stretched out across the seat. It was Christmas Eve. Tomorrow their passes expired. When they didn't return home, their owners would know they had escaped and would send the slave hunters after them. What if there were delays and they didn't reach Philadelphia in time?

At Petersburg, Virginia, her restless nap was disturbed by an older man and his two young daughters. "Please, sir, don't," said the darker-haired daughter as Ellen made room for her on the couch. "Stay there and rest yourself."

And avoid conversation, too, thought Ellen.

"Would you like my shawl for a pillow?" the girl offered.

"Take mine, too," offered the other daughter.

Good old Southern hospitality. Ellen lay back on the couch and pretended to sleep. Her eyes were closed, but she sensed the girls' eyes on her. After a while she got up.

"May I be so bold, sir, as to ask what ails you?" said the father.

"Inflammatory rheumatism, sir."

"I know it well." The man took out a pencil and paper and began writing.

"Where are you going, sir?" asked the dark-haired daughter. Ellen felt the girls' eyes trying to penetrate her dark glasses.

"Hush now, girls," the father reproached his daughters gently. "This gentleman's got a lot on his mind." He offered a paper to Ellen. "Sir, this recipe is the perfect cure for rheumatism. Always put it on when I feel a touch coming."

Ellen would have gladly faked reading the perfect cure to make the man happy, but since she couldn't read, she didn't know which way to hold the paper. She thanked him profusely and tucked it into her waistcoat pocket.

At Richmond the gentleman and his daughters got off the train, and a stout, elderly woman and a young man took their seats. No sooner was the woman seated than she sprang up and pulled down the window. "There goes my nigger, Ned! That no-good runaway!"

Poor Ned! Ellen looked out the window. Her heart sank. William was walking on the platform. The woman had mistaken him for her slave. "No, that's my boy," she said nervously.

"Ned, you come back here, you rascal!" the woman shouted at William.

"Madam, that's *my* boy, William, not your Ned!"

The woman drew her head in. "I beg your pardon, sir. I was so sure it was my nigger. Never in my life saw two black pigs more alike than your boy and my Ned."

The train pulled away from the station. The woman leaned back in the seat and closed her eyes. "Sir, I hope your boy won't turn out to be as worthless as my Ned. I was as kind to him as if he had been my own son. It grieves me to think that after all I did for him, he ran off."

"When did he leave you?" asked the man.

"About eighteen months ago. A few months after I sold his wife." She sighed. "She was as good and faithful a nigger as you could wish for. And beautiful too. . . . Whiter than I am. Whiter than both of you."

"Then why did you sell her?" asked the man.

"Had to. The poor thing got so ill she couldn't work."

The man waited a minute before he spoke again. "Since she was *so* faithful, and served you *so* well, why didn't you free her so she could live out her sickly life in a bit of ease?"

"Freeing niggers is the worst thing you can do for them. Just before my dear husband died, he decided to free ours. I knew he wasn't in his right mind to do that, so I had the will changed back." She pursed her lips and shook her head back and forth, like Mrs. Collins did when she was getting ready to complain about something. "Niggers are more trouble than they're worth. Ten of mine have run away since my poor husband died."

Lord keep them free, thought Ellen.

"My son, poor boy, he lives up north now, in New York. He says that my slaves are much better off than the free ones there."

"Then I have no doubt that your Ned and the other nine will realize their mistake and return home." Ellen felt that the man was holding back laughing.

An hour later, when the woman left the train, the man turned to Ellen. "Damn shame. That old bag cheating those poor Negroes out of their liberty."

Ellen liked him but refrained from further conversation.

At Washington, D.C., William and Ellen took the train for Baltimore, Maryland. When they arrived, William went to check that their luggage would follow them to Philadelphia.

"Where you going, boy?" A military officer blocked his way.

William sprang to attention. "Philadelphia, sir."

"What are you going there for?"

"Goin' with my master, sir."

"Bring him to me, boy. And be quick about it. Your train's ready to leave."

William ran to get Ellen who was seated in

the crowded waiting room. "Master, a gentleman would like to see you." His voice was calm, but fear showed in his eyes. She leaned on him to get up, and he led her to the officer.

"My boy told me you wanted to see me." Ellen was afraid, but they were so close to freedom she wasn't going to let this bully ruin everything.

"Yes, sir. It's against our rules, sir, to allow anyone to take a slave out of Baltimore into Philadelphia unless we're satisfied that he has a right to do so."

"Why is that?"

"Because if the gentleman traveling with the slave turns out *not* to be his rightful owner, and if the rightful owner comes here and proves that his slave got through here, law says we have to pay him for the slave."

"Isn't it obvious that I am a slaveholder?" she said indignantly.

"Of course it's obvious," said an interested passenger.

"Let him go," said another passenger. "Can't you see he's an invalid?"

"I bought my tickets in Charleston," Ellen continued in the same angry tone. "They questioned me there at length. You have no right to do so now."

"Well, sir, right or wrong, I'm doing it."

"This is ridiculous . . . and insulting." She summoned up the arrogance she had heard all her life.

"Do you know anyone in Baltimore who could vouch for you?"

"Ask that man over there." She pointed haughtily to the conductor of the train they had been on.

The man hurried over to the conductor. The bell rang for the train. *Please, dear Lord.*

The officer hurried back. "I guess it's all right for you to go. Your being so ill and all. And the conductor remembers you well."

"I would hope so." Ellen hobbled across the platform as quickly as possible. William helped her into one of the first-class carriages, then ran along the platform looking for the car for free coloreds and slaves. There was none. He ended up in the luggage car. Tiredness caught up with him, and he fell asleep.

Ellen drifted off for a few hours, but when she awakened, it was dark and cold. She felt scared. She rang for the conductor. "Can you find my boy?"

"Haven't seen him for some time."

"Find him for me," she ordered.

"I'm no slave hunter."

"Call the porter," she said firmly.

The porter found William in the luggage car. "Wake up. Your master's looking for you." He laughed. "That white man sure is scared." He lowered his voice to a whisper. "Brother, we're pulling into Philadelphia. I'll tell him I didn't find you, and I'll hide you till he leaves the station."

"Can't do that to my master. He need me more than anyone."

"Are you mad? One nigger's the same to a white man as another." William didn't respond.

The porter shook his head in disbelief. "Well, if you change your mind, go to Thirty-one North Fifth Street. They'll be real friendly to you."

"I remember that. Thank you, brother."

The bell clanged as they pulled into the station. William hurried through the cars to find Ellen. No one paid attention as the husky black man helped his invalid master off the train. No one heard him hail a carriage and confidently tell the driver, "Thirty-one North Fifth Street, please."

Abolitionist William Lloyd Garrison wrote up the Crafts' daring escape in his newspaper The Liberator, *and the Crafts began telling their story in cities and towns across the United States. In 1850, fearing that they could be captured and returned to their masters under the provisions of the soon-to-be passed Fugitive Slave Act, they moved to England. After the Civil War they returned to the United States, bought a former Georgia plantation and set up a school for black children and adults.*

AFTERWORD

When I began researching stories for this book, I knew of only a few black conductors on the Underground Railroad such as ex-slaves Harriet Tubman and William Wells Brown, and abolitionist leader Robert Purvis. Tubman's feats are legendary; she risked her life, returning at least fifteen times into the slave states to bring out more than one hundred slaves. William Wells Brown, who became a well-known antislavery speaker, wrote a book about his escape and offered his home in Buffalo, New York, as a stop on the Underground Railroad. Robert Purvis was a founder of the American Anti-Slavery Society in 1833 and President of the Philadelphia Vigilance

Committee for ten years. In his house he built a special room, reached only by a trap door, to hide runaways.

Through my research, I discovered how active and dominant black Americans were in creating and sustaining the efforts of the Underground Railroad. Citizens in free black settlements such as Cabin Creek, Indiana, and Sandusky, Ohio, and in cities such as Richmond, Virginia, Cincinnati, Ohio, St. Louis, Missouri, and Boston, Massachusetts, hid runaways, helped them get farther north and into Canada, found them jobs and helped them settle down. Free blacks paddled runaways in their skiffs across the Ohio River from Kentucky to Indiana. Black porters on trains and workers on ships smuggled fugitives. Wealthy blacks such as Chicago's John Jones and Philadelphia's Dr. James J. Bias welcomed fugitives into their homes. Runaways, like Lewis Hayden from Kentucky, constantly courted danger by providing refuge to fugitives. When Ellen Craft's owner sent bounty hunters to Boston after her and William, Hayden hid William in his home.

Like their white counterparts, these black conductors risked fines and imprisonment for helping fugitives. In Washington, D.C., Leonard A. Grimes, who transported paying passengers in his horse-drawn carriages and took runaways for free, was caught taking a slave family out of Virginia and imprisoned for two years. James A. Smith spent seven years in prison for helping other slaves not as lucky as Henry Box Brown.

Blacks in Pennsylvania, New York, Massachusetts, and Michigan formed Vigilance Committees; these groups provided food, shelter and money to the fugitives and letters of introduction to help them find jobs. David Ruggles headed the predominantly black New York Committee of Vigilance. Frederick Douglass was among the hundreds of runaways helped by Ruggles.

A Vigilance Committee composed of eleven whites and two blacks was founded in Philadelphia in 1838. Robert Purvis was its president and Jacob C. White, who was also black, its executive secretary. When the group reorganized in 1844, seven of its nineteen leaders were black. Purvis was elected chairman, and William Still became executive secretary. From December 1852 to February 1857, under Still's leadership, the committee helped 495 fugitives.

Still set out to document the courage and daring of these slaves and to provide a record that might help them find other members of their families. In 1872 he published *The Underground Rail Road*, accounts of over 800 escapes of men, women and children. These stories of courage and cunning found a ready public. The first edition of 10,000 copies sold out. Two subsequent editions in 1879 and 1883 also sold well.

In choosing the stories for this book, I concentrated on individual acts of courage by slaves determined to be free at any cost. I also focused on the role played by free blacks and other abolitionists who risked imprisonment to help others achieve freedom. Original accounts of these stories are found in the sources that follow.

The River of Ice

This story was recounted in *Reminiscences of Levi Coffin*. Coffin's antislavery activities earned him the nickname President of the Underground Railroad; Coffin and his wife, Catherine, sheltered over 3,000 runaways at their home in Newport (now Fountain City), Indiana.

Eliza's escape was written up in many antislavery newspapers. Her courage and desperation so moved Harriet Beecher Stowe that she made her a central character called Eliza in her antislavery novel *Uncle Tom's Cabin*. While Coffin, in telling this story, referred to Eliza Harris as the runaway, other accounts led me to believe that perhaps this was not her real name. I chose the name Caroline for her daughter.

Free Like the Wind

This story was recounted in Coffin's *Reminiscences* and also in a pamphlet, *The Economy-*

Cabin Creek Short Branch and Some of Its Operatives by C. E. Charles.

A *Shipment of Dry Goods*

In 1849, with the help of a friend, Henry Brown wrote about his life and escape in *Narrative of Henry Box Brown . . . by Himself.* William Still also wrote about Henry's escape in *The Underground Rail Road.* It was in Still's account that I learned that Henry recited Psalm 40 to the abolitionists.

Pretending

Passmore Williamson wrote a pamphlet explaining his part in Jane Johnson's case. The *New York Daily Tribune* followed the case from Johnson's escape to Williamson's release from prison. This story was also recounted in William Still's *The Underground Rail Road.*

"Two Tickets for Mr. Johnson and Slave"

With the help of a friend, William Craft wrote about the escape in *Running a Thousand Miles for Freedom*. Some of the dialogue in this version is taken from Craft's account of his wife's conversations with passengers on the trip north.

Acknowledgments

I thank Dorothy Carter of the Bank Street College of Education for offering her insights and experience in evaluating the manuscript; Wilma Dulin, Archivist at the Indiana Historical Society, who answered my many requests for pertinent materials; and my editor, Katherine Brown Tegen, for her continued humor and support.

SELECTED BIBLIOGRAPHY

*Starred books were written for young readers.

Bontemps, Arna. *Great Slave Narratives.* Boston: Beacon Press, 1969.

Charles, C. E. *The Economy-Cabin Creek Short Branch and Some of Its Operatives.* Indiana: Society of Indiana Pioneers, 1971.

Craft, William. *Running a Thousand Miles for Freedom.* London: 1860. Reprint: New York: Arno Press, 1969.

Coffin, Levi. *Reminiscences of Levi Coffin.* New York: Arno Press, 1968.

*Hamilton, Virginia. *Anthony Burns: The Defeat and Triumph of a Fugitive Slave.* New York: Knopf, 1988.

*Hansen, Joyce. *Out of This Place*. New York: Walker & Company, 1988.

*———*Which Way Freedom?* New York: Walker & Company, 1986.

*Lester, Julius. *Long Journey Home*. New York: Scholastic, 1988.

*———*This Strange New Feeling*. New York: Dial Books, 1982.

*———*To Be a Slave*. New York: Scholastic, 1986.

*Levine, Ellen. *If You Traveled on the Underground Railroad*. New York: Scholastic, 1988.

*Meltzer, Milton. *The Black Americans: A History in Their Own Words*. New York: Crowell, 1987.

*Petry, Ann. *Harriet Tubman: Conductor on the Underground Railroad*. New York: Archway, 1977.

Quarles, Benjamin. *Black Abolitionists*. New York: Oxford University Press, 1969.

Siebert, Wilbur. *The Underground Railroad in Massachusetts*. Worcester: American Antiquarian Society, 1936.

*Smucker, Barbara. *Runaway to Freedom: A Story of the Underground Railway* New York: Harper & Row, 1979.

Sterling, Dorothy. *Black Foremothers: Three Lives*. Westbury, NY: Feminist Press, 1988.

*———*Freedom Train: The Story of Harriet Tubman*. New York: Scholastic, 1987.

Still, William. *The Underground Rail Road*. Philadelphia: Porter and Coates, 1872. Reprint: New York: Arno Press, 1968.

*Warner, Lucille Schulberg. *From Slave to Abolitionist: The Life of William Wells Brown*. New York: Dial Books, 1976.

Weld, Theodore D. *American Slavery As It Is: Testimony of a Thousand Witnesses*. New York: American Anti-Slavery Society, 1839.

Williamson, Passmore. *Case of Passmore Williamson: Report of the Proceedings in the Writ of Habeas Corpus, Issued by J. K. Kane in the Case of the U.S. of A., ex. re. J. H. Wheeler vs. P. Williamson*. Philadelphia: U. Hunt and Son, 1856.